ALSO IN THE BLASTA BOOKS SERIES

blastabooks.com

WHOLE CATCH

Written by Aishling Moore

Illustrated by Nicky Hooper

CONTENTS

INTRODUCTION

The whole-catch approach is the baseline concept for what we wanted to do when we opened Goldie, our seafood restaurant in Cork City, in 2019. We wanted to serve the fish that had previously been thrown back and that continues to be exported out of Ireland. We wanted to convert the wary to fully fledged seafood lovers.

Our menu was almost completely dictated by what the local boats landed. In the early days, I literally would not know what fish I'd be working with until the delivery came in. It was a rock 'n' roll time. We wanted to commit to whatever was landed and use as much of that as possible, so we began serving crunchy fish spines, smoked fish collars, taramasalata and fish head terrines.

We also had to find ways to prepare and store kilos of whole fish without using cling film or single-use plastic because these are the types of issues you want to be tackling in your first year of business. We had to plan and prepare for bad weather with no boats out, so we also had to build up a larder that we could still open the restaurant with to challenge the idea of the 'catch of the day'.

Yet there are many rewards from preparing a whole fish yourself. Perhaps most importantly, you are taking responsibility for the whole animal. Buying and storing fish whole has many benefits, improved shelf life being the most notable. I developed my method for prepping round fish out of necessity when we were a new business with no walk-in and an 80kg mix of highly perishable fish that don't typically feature on Irish menus.

Fillets are for main courses and everything else must be for, well, everything else. So we fried the tails in a buttermilk batter, salted the trim and emulsified it with potato and olive oil, smoked the roe, glazed the collars, picked the head meat, and battered the tongues and cheeks in buckwheat. These all became the real stars of our menus, which change every day.

SUSTAINABLE FISH

There is more information available than ever on how fisheries are managed, how quotas are decided, what fishing methods are used and when spawning seasons begin and end. This information overload has perhaps complicated the decisions we make when it comes to what fish we buy, cook and eat. We want to be told, 'Eat [fill in the blank] and you're a good person making informed choices that safeguard our oceans' future.' However, the answer is not one species, but rather, every species. The single best thing you can do to eat fish responsibly and sustainably is to eat a wide variety of fish.

 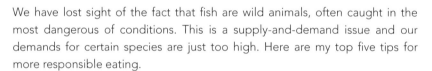

The single best thing you can do to eat fish responsibly and sustainably is to eat a wide variety of fish.

We have lost sight of the fact that fish are wild animals, often caught in the most dangerous of conditions. This is a supply-and-demand issue and our demands for certain species are just too high. Here are my top five tips for more responsible eating.

1 Eat a wide variety of wild species.

2 Support regenerative aquaculture by eating more oysters and mussels (see page 26 for more on this).

3 Shop locally – the shorter the supply chain, the better. Develop a relationship with your local fishmonger and don't be afraid to ask questions.

4 Be aware that poor weather conditions will limit the variety on offer.

5 If you're eating out in a restaurant and see a species on the menu you haven't tried before, order it.

ESSENTIAL EQUIPMENT

1 **SHARP, FLEXIBLE FILLETING KNIFE** With one of these you can tackle almost any whole fish, but it *must* be sharp. If you are weary of knife sharpening, bring your knife to a cobbler. Blunt knives are actually more dangerous than sharp knives and are incompatible with whole fish preparation.

2 **KITCHEN SHEARS OR SCISSORS** Fundamental for removing fins and for cutting and trimming bones.

3 **JAPANESE SCALER** This is a fantastic investment as it causes little to no damage to the fish. You can find Japanese scrapers in most kitchenware shops online, but if you can't source one, you can use an old, blunt knife.

4 **PIN BONER** Many of our methods for whole fish preparation were developed to reduce the amount of time spent pin boning, i.e. plucking the smaller bones of the fish with a tweezer-like tool. These bones are most often found running down the centre of a fish fillet. We cut through or around bones for both efficiency and to preserve the flesh. Pin boning often damages the fish, especially if the flesh hasn't been salted or cured beforehand. However, a pin boner is essential for processing many fish like mackerel, gurnard and red mullet.

5 **DOUGH SCRAPER** When prepping whole fish, a dough scraper is indispensable for keeping your work surface or chopping board clean and dry. It will dramatically cut down on the amount of kitchen paper you use.

BUYING & STORING FISH

BUYING FISH

① Fresh fish should appear rigid. The flesh should be firmly fixed to the frame, like a tailor-made suit.

② Fresh fish should smell of the sea.

③ Pay special attention to the eyes when buying fish – they should be plump and bulging.

④ Fish covered in slime or mucus is actually a good sign of freshness. This slime is a glycoprotein that actively prevents bacteria and parasites from attaching to the skin.

⑤ The gills located just behind the head should be bright red and shiny.

⑥ Always ask your fishmonger what they'd recommend.

⑦ Trust your senses.

⑧ Refrigeration is essential to the shelf life of fresh fish, so make it the last stop on your shopping trip.

STORING FISH

1 The correct storage and handling of fish is more crucial to deliciousness than the cooking.

2 Fish should ideally be stored between 0°C and 2°C.

3 Remove fish from the refrigerator at least 15 minutes before cooking. This allows for more even cooking.

4 If possible, store fish on the bone. This limits exposure to bacteria and prevents the leaching of moisture, which causes spoilage to occur more quickly. For example, we've had great success hanging monkfish tails on the bone for two-plus days. Once removed from the bone, the fish automatically begins releasing moisture, which is something we are always trying to avoid.

5 Store fish gutted and with heads removed. This will slow down the deterioration of the fish. It will also save you some storage space. When gutting fish prior to storage, do so carefully so that you don't perforate any of the innards. Wipe the cavity clean with kitchen paper.

6 Remove fish, whether whole or filleted, from its packaging and pat it dry with kitchen paper before storing it in the fridge.

7 Never store raw fish in or on plastic, as this encourages the fish to sweat.

8 Never wash fish with water. Moisture drastically speeds up the deterioration of the fish.

9 Store your fish flat on a tray or a plate with space in between the whole fish or fillets. Good air circulation between the fillets is so important – it affects the freshness and how it will cook. Good air circulation keeps fish fresher for longer and inhibits the fish from leaching moisture, which impacts the cooking process.

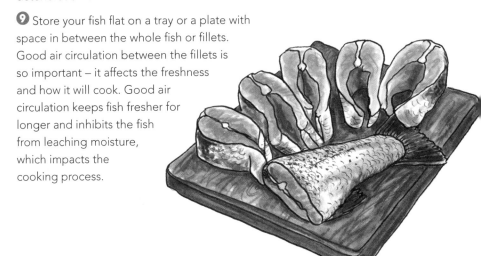

GOLDIE'S WHOLE-CATCH IRISH MENU

SHELLFISH
Brown crab

Clams

Cockles

Crayfish

Langoustines

Lobsters

Mussels

Oysters

Periwinkles

Scallops

Shrimp

Spider crab

FLAT FISH
Dover sole

Halibut

John Dory

Lemon sole

Megrim

Plaice

Slip sole

Turbot

Witches

ROUND FISH
Cod

Haddock

Hake

Ling

Pollock

Whiting

OILY FISH
Blackwater salmon

Bonito

Grey mullet

Red mullet

Sardines

Tuna

OTHERS
Gurnard

Monkfish

Ray/skate

Shad

Squid

Stone bass

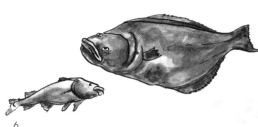

HOW TO
PREPARE A
WHOLE MACKEREL

If you're new to the preparation of whole fish, mackerel is a great one to start with. It doesn't require scaling, it's small compared to round fish and it's also relatively inexpensive, so there is less pressure if you mess it up.

This is my preferred method for preparing mackerel. Leaving the head on and guts intact makes the process faster but also reduces the need to wash the fillets once removed from the frame of the fish.

1 Secure your chopping board with a damp kitchen cloth on a sanitised work surface so that it doesn't move around as you work.

2 Put the mackerel on the chopping board. Wipe it with some kitchen paper to remove excess moisture.

3 Make an incision behind the pectoral fins at each side of the mackerel. The pectoral fins sit just behind the head.

4 Using these incisions as a guide, place your knife at the exit point of the cut parallel to the backbone of the fish.

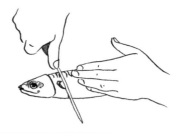

5 To expose the first fillet, work from the head to the tail of the fish. Placing your knife as close as possible to the backbone of the fish, run the knife along the spine in one sweeping motion, gliding through the bones that attach the fillet to the frame of the fish.

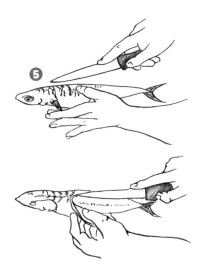

6 To expose the second fillet, turn the mackerel over on its side. Make a small incision across the tail end of the fillet to help, then repeat the same action as in step 5, but this time working from the tail to the head.

7 Trim the fillets, removing any remnants of the innards.

8 Discard the head and guts.

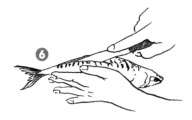

9 To make pin-boning the fish easier, use your filleting knife to make two delicate incisions at 20° angles at either side of the bones running down the centre of the fish. Be careful not to slice through the skin.

10 Using a pin boner, remove the bones from the fish, working as delicately as possible so that you don't damage the flesh of the fillets.

TANDOORI MACKEREL WITH GHERKIN & CAPER RAITA

SERVES 4

The robust flavour of mackerel stands up well to the tandoori marinade, which also acts as a non-stick barrier between the fish and the pan. I usually avoid serving oily fish such as mackerel with dairy, but the lactic acid in the yogurt complements the fattiness of the fish.

4 whole mackerel, filleted and pin-boned (or 8 fillets)

FOR THE MARINADE:

1 garlic clove, grated

a small thumb-sized piece of fresh ginger, peeled and grated

juice of 1 lime

2 tbsp vegetable oil

1 tsp garam masala

½ tsp ground cumin

½ tsp ground coriander

½ tsp ground turmeric

¼ tsp cayenne pepper

150g full-fat natural yogurt

To make the raita, combine all the ingredients in a small bowl. Taste and season with sea salt and a little more lemon juice if needed. Set aside until you're ready to serve.

To make the marinade, blend the garlic, ginger, lime juice, oil and spices using a handheld blender or a food processor, then add to the yogurt in a small bowl and mix to combine. This can be made ahead and keeps well in the fridge for up to a week.

Preheat the oven to 200°C (180°C fan). Lightly grease a baking tray with vegetable oil.

Score the mackerel fillets with a sharp knife. To do this, pinch the fillet and make shallow incisions in the centre, being careful not to slice through it. Scoring the fish speeds up the cooking time, prevents the fillets from curling as they cook and allows the marinade to penetrate through the fish.

Put the mackerel fillets on a baking tray or a plate, skin side up. Using a pastry brush, spread the marinade over the skin of the mackerel and season with salt.

Heat a stainless steel frying pan on a medium-high heat. Working in batches, put the mackerel in the pan, marinade side down. The fillets may curl up as they hit the pan – if they do, use a spatula to apply some pressure, flattening them out to ensure even caramelisation on the surface. As soon as the fillets retract from the pan, turn the heat down to medium and cook for 2–3 minutes, until 60% of the flesh side of the mackerel has turned from pink to opaque.

**FOR THE GHERKIN
& CAPER RAITA:**

250g full-fat natural yogurt

65g gherkins, diced

juice of 1 lemon

1 tbsp chopped fresh dill

2 tsp capers, chopped

¼ tsp ground cumin

¼ tsp ground coriander

a pinch of fine sea salt

Remove the fillets from the pan and put them on the greased baking tray. Once all the fillets have been seared, transfer the tray to the preheated oven for 2 minutes to finish cooking.

Remove the fillets from the oven and serve immediately with the raita.

SHIME MACKEREL

SERVES 4

Mackerel is one of the most nutritious and versatile fish our waters have to offer. This Japanese preparation is mostly used for sashimi, but it's my favourite method to use when mackerel is at its peak. This recipe preserves the texture of the raw fatty flesh by way of salt, vinegar and mirin. The addition of kombu kelp seaweed subtly reinforces the umami taste of the fish. Kombu can be purchased in Asian supermarkets or health food shops or you can forage for it.

2 whole mackerel
(or 4 fillets)

fine sea salt

80ml rice wine vinegar

80ml mirin

10g dried kombu kelp
seaweed (see the intro)

TO SERVE:

wasabi

soy sauce

To prepare whole mackerel, follow the steps on pages 8–9 but **do not pin-bone the mackerel**. You'll do this at the end of the curing process. This curing method tightens the flesh, which causes the bones running down the centre of the fish to protrude. This makes pin-boning much easier and causes less damage to the flesh.

After the fillets have been removed from the frame of the mackerel, quickly rinse them in a bowl of ice-cold water. Pat the fillets dry with kitchen paper.

Lay the mackerel fillets skin side down on a stainless steel tray. Sprinkle each of the fillets with some fine sea salt.

Combine the rice wine vinegar, mirin and kombu in a small bowl. Pour this mixture over the mackerel and refrigerate for 10 hours, uncovered.

Remove the mackerel from the marinade and discard the kombu. Pat the mackerel dry and pin-bone each fillet.

Turn the fillets flesh side down. Working from the head end of the fish, delicately pull the skin away from the fillets. Plenty of fish have a somewhat 'plasticky' outer skin on top of the skin that we recognise the fish by. This outer membrane requires cooking, so removing it here makes for more pleasurable eating. The same thing goes for red mullet when eating it raw.

Using a sharp knife, cut the mackerel into thin slices across the fillets. Eat within 24 hours and serve with wasabi and soy sauce.

SEAWEED

Seaweed is a food of our past and present and is sure to be a huge food source for the future. It's used in cosmetics, as fertilizer, as biomass for fuel and as a setting agent in jellies. We have hundreds of varieties of seaweed in Ireland. Foraging for some of these seaweeds is a beautiful way to spend a morning or afternoon. Seaweed foraging in Ireland is typically best done between March and October.

Seaweed adds deep umami and meaty flavours to so many dishes and is an incredible seasoning for everything from tomatoes to spuds. It's also a fantastic substitute for salt.

1 KOMBU KELP Most notably used in dashi broth, kombu adds deep layers of flavour to any stock or sauce.

2 NORI Nori (or *sleabhan* in Irish) is my favourite seaweed to dry and use in seasonings. Nori has a fabulous grassiness and an amazing nuttiness when toasted. We slice potatoes wafer thin on a mandolin and deep-fry them at 160°C, season them with nori powder and sea salt and serve them as a snack with some cultured cream.

3 DILLISK This seaweed has a distinctive purple hue, so it's easily recognisable. I love this seaweed pickled in equal quantities of apple cider vinegar, sugar and water.

4 CARRAGEEN MOSS This seaweed is used all over the world as a setting agent and is the key ingredient in Myrtle Allen's famous carrageen moss pudding at Ballymaloe House. It's also pescatarian, vegetarian and vegan friendly for those looking for gelatine substitutes.

5 PEPPER DULSE Also known as sea truffle for its black garlic flavour profile, this seaweed is delicious when just picked and retains its flavour well when dried.

TOP FORAGING TIPS

1 Before you go foraging, check the tide timetable as well as the water quality of the area (this information is all accessible online).

2 Cut the seaweed using a pocket knife or scissors.

3 Always keep the roots of the plant attached to the rocks to allow the seaweed to replenish.

HOW TO
PREPARE A WHOLE HAKE

An average fish has two fillets and a tail. Depending on the species and the season, it might also have two cheeks and an extractable and palatable tongue, roe and liver. This method for preparing round fish removes the fins, scales, head, belly and tail first while allowing you to store the prize fillets on the bone in your fridge. We call these saddles. Two days on the bone in the fridge allows the skin to dry out and removes excess water, making it much easier to remove the fillets from the bone, and develops the flavour. The length of time we can store the fish like this depends on many factors: when it was caught, when it was landed, when it was delivered, the size of the fish, the time of year and how much storage space we have.

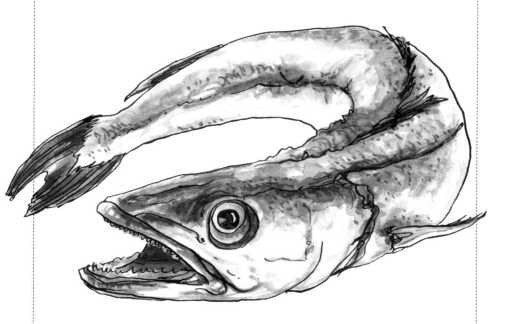

I'm using hake here, but this method works for any round fish.

1 Secure your chopping board with a damp kitchen cloth on a sanitised work surface so that it doesn't move around as you work.

2 Put the hake on the chopping board. Wipe the fish with some kitchen paper to remove any slime and excess moisture.

3 Using kitchen scissors, remove the dorsal and anal fins. Discard.

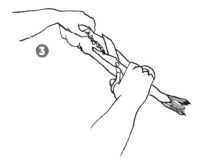

4 Put the chopping board in the sink at an angle. Put the whole hake on the chopping board with its head pointing away from you and hold the tail of the fish with your non-dominant hand (i.e. the hand you don't write with). Put some kitchen paper around the tail to secure your grip.

5 Using sweeping movements, run the scaler all around the surface area of the fish, working from the tail down towards the head to remove the scales. Don't use any extra force, which would damage the fish skin and lacerate the flesh.

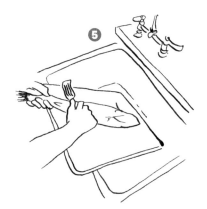

6 This is messy work but resist the temptation to use water to remove the scales as you work. Excess moisture will make the fish deteriorate more quickly.

7 Scrape the scales off the chopping board using a dough scraper. Using kitchen paper, wipe off any loose scales that remain on the surface of the fish. Dispose of the scales.

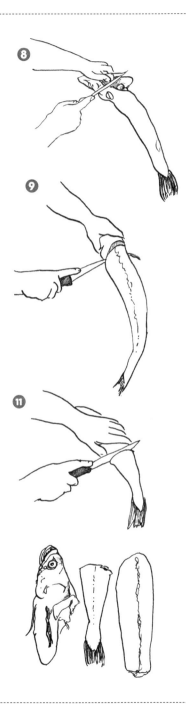

8 Put the chopping board back on the damp kitchen cloth. Now you're going to detach the collars of the fish on both sides. Do this at an angle to achieve two triangle-shaped collars. Using scissors, remove the collars from the fish and set aside.

9 Remove the head and set it aside. (A fish rots from the head down, so that's always the first thing you want to cook, serve or remove if you intend to store the fish for more than a day.)

10 Trim the belly on both sides of the fish. This will aid the removal of excess water and allow air to circulate around the fillets.

11 To remove the tail, cut through the frame of the fish by placing your knife at the starting point of the anal fin behind the stomach cavity. Set the tail aside.

12 Wipe the saddle well with kitchen paper. Store it in the fridge on a stainless steel tray or a large plate, uncovered, to dry out. I like to leave the saddle in the refrigerator for at least 12 hours before removing the fillets. This makes it much easier to remove the fillets without damaging the fish.

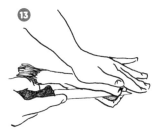

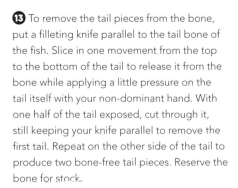

13 To remove the tail pieces from the bone, put a filleting knife parallel to the tail bone of the fish. Slice in one movement from the top to the bottom of the tail to release it from the bone while applying a little pressure on the tail itself with your non-dominant hand. With one half of the tail exposed, cut through it, still keeping your knife parallel to remove the first tail. Repeat on the other side of the tail to produce two bone-free tail pieces. Reserve the bone for stock.

14 To remove the fillets from the bone, put the saddle of the hake on your chopping board with the backbone facing upright and the stomach cavity sitting parallel to the board.

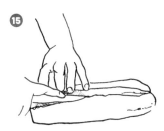

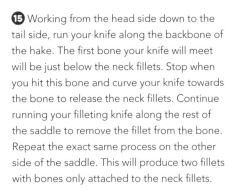

15 Working from the head side down to the tail side, run your knife along the backbone of the hake. The first bone your knife will meet will be just below the neck fillets. Stop when you hit this bone and curve your knife towards the bone to release the neck fillets. Continue running your filleting knife along the rest of the saddle to remove the fillet from the bone. Repeat the exact same process on the other side of the saddle. This will produce two fillets with bones only attached to the neck fillets.

16 Slice through the fillets to remove the neck fillets and cut away the bones to the side of the fillets. Depending on the size of the fish, I like to cut these neck fillets into three pieces, which together are enough for one serving.

17 Portion the main hake fillets in two (depending on the size of the fish), trimming away any remaining innards.

KARAAGE HAKE NUGGETS

SERVES 4

Preparing whole fish leaves you with a lot more than the fillet, so you'll rarely find a menu at Goldie that doesn't feature some type of nugget as a snack. Karaage is a Japanese method of deep-frying where the food (usually meat or fish) is marinated before being coated in a starch and fried. This recipe is perfect for the trim from any round fish but it also works particularly well with the meatiness of monkfish.

500g hake tails or trim, diced into 2cm cubes or nuggets

vegetable oil, for deep-frying

1 egg white, beaten

135g potato starch

FOR THE MARINADE:

3 garlic cloves, finely grated

1 tsp finely grated fresh ginger

5 tbsp soy sauce

3 tbsp sake

¼ tsp caster sugar

TO SERVE:

togarashi mayo (page 60)

Mix all the marinade ingredients together in a large bowl. Add the hake nuggets, tossing to coat the fish in the marinade. Refrigerate for 25 minutes.

Heat the oil in a deep-fryer to 180°C (or see the tip on page 20 if you don't have a deep-fryer).

Drain the nuggets from the marinade and transfer to a clean mixing bowl. Add the beaten egg white to the nuggets and toss to coat.

Put the potato starch in a wide, shallow bowl. Working in batches, toss the nuggets through the potato starch, shaking off the excess as you go.

Working in batches, fry the nuggets for about 2 minutes, until golden brown. Drain on kitchen paper and serve immediately with togarashi mayo.

BUTTERMILK FRIED HAKE TAILS

SERVES 4

This recipe works well with any round or flat fish. This is one of my favourite ways to use the tails of round fish, but you can use any part of a fillet of round fish. This is best served with lime mayonnaise, bread and butter pickles and an extra splash of hot sauce. Add a couple of brioche buns and some shredded iceberg lettuce and you have the makings of a serious fish sambo.

vegetable oil, for deep-frying

350g hake tails, removed from the bone

180g plain flour

½ tsp fine sea salt

150ml buttermilk

1 tbsp hot sauce (page 65 or shop-bought), plus extra to serve

TO SERVE:

lime mayonnaise (page 60)

bread and butter pickles (page 62)

TOP TIP

If you don't have a deep-fryer, use a heavy-based pot or casserole, fill it no more than halfway with oil and work in small batches. A thermometer is essential if you don't have a deep-fryer.

Preheat the oil in a deep-fryer to 180°C (or see the tip if you don't have a deep-fryer).

Remove the skin from the hake and discard it, then cut the tails into fingers 2cm wide x 12cm long. This should give you approx. 12 fish fingers.

Put the flour and salt in a medium-sized mixing bowl and stir to combine.

Put the buttermilk and hot sauce in a separate mixing bowl and mix well.

Add 1 tablespoon of the buttermilk and hot sauce mixture to the flour and mix it through, forming little clumps throughout the flour. This will result in a crispier, crunchier coating on the fish.

Working in batches, add the fish to the flour mixture and toss to coat. Shake off any excess flour, then dip each piece in the buttermilk and hot sauce mixture. Drain off the excess liquid and return once more to the flour mixture, coating well and again shaking off the excess flour. Transfer the fish to a plate or baking tray, ready for frying. I don't like to do this ahead of time, as the buttermilk and hot sauce will start to break down the fish.

Working in batches (I do no more than four pieces at a time), deep-fry the coated fish for 2 minutes, until golden brown. Drain on kitchen paper, sprinkle with sea salt and anoint with more hot sauce to serve with the lime mayo and bread and butter pickles.

NON-STICK TIPS FOR COOKING FISH

I meet lovers of fish, food and cooking every day, yet these same people are often reluctant to cook fish at home because they are afraid the fillet will stick to the pan. Although delicious, effective and efficient, pan-frying is not always the best way to cook every piece of fish. But when you do pan-fry a beautiful piece of fish, here are my top non-stick hacks.

1 DRY YOUR FISH Ensuring the fish you are cooking is free from excess moisture is the most vital factor to consider when cooking fish regardless of the cooking method, but particularly when pan-frying. The combination of water and oil will prevent a crispy exterior or skin from forming, which is what you want when pan-frying. See also page 5 on how to store fish.

2 TEMPERATURE Temperature control is essential to successful cooking. In fact, it's so important that it's second only to the product and the treatment of that product prior to cooking, which includes drying your fish. When pan-frying fish, preheat the pan for 1½–2 minutes on a medium-high heat before adding any oil. This will give you a cooking surface with even heat distribution. Use a flavourless vegetable oil such as sunflower or rapeseed oil, as these have a higher smoke point (the smoke point refers to the temperature at which the oil you are cooking with begins to burn). Don't overcrowd the pan. Each addition to a cooking surface reduces the temperature of the pan. Overcrowding also causes the food in the pan to steam, creating undesirable water.

3 PANS Stainless steel frying pans are my preference for cooking fish. They require little to no maintenance, they conduct and distribute heat quickly and evenly, and they don't come with a long list of rules for upkeep.

4 PARCHMENT This is an incredibly useful hack for non-stick frying. Cut a square of parchment paper that's bigger than the surface area of the piece(s) of fish you're cooking but small enough to fit on the cooking surface of your frying pan. Heat your pan and add some oil, then put the parchment in the pan, ensuring the base is lightly covered in oil and the paper is flush to the cooking surface. Add a little more oil on top of the parchment, then put your fish directly on the oiled parchment to cook. If using this method, pay particular attention to the temperature of the pan, as the parchment can burn.

CREAM PLAIN
FLOUR

5 FLOUR Lightly coating fish in plain flour was the only way I had seen fresh fish cooked in my house as a child (other than fish fingers, of course). It's a classic cooking method with origins in France and is still relevant today. This technique is especially useful when pan-frying flat fish with delicate skin, like lemon sole, or with no skin, like Dover sole. Make sure to pat the fish dry before coating it lightly in flour, then tap off as much excess flour as possible.

7 OTHER COOKING METHODS
Poaching is a great option for sea trout, cod and monkfish. Baking fish in the oven is a truly underrated option for cooking fish. This works well with red mullet, turbot, plaice and pretty much any round fish. Preheat the oven to 180°C (160°C fan). Melt a couple tablespoons of butter. Brush the fish and the base of a baking tray with the melted butter. Season the fish with sea salt and bake in the preheated oven for 5–6 minutes for a flat filleted fish or 8–10 minutes for a round filleted fish. Invest in a small bamboo steamer – it's great for cooking thick pieces of cod, halibut, brill and turbot. Put a little oiled piece of parchment paper on the base of the steamer before putting the fish on top. Add lots of aromatics like onions, herbs, spices and lemon zest to the water to season the fish as it cooks.

6 COATINGS, CRUSTS & MARINADES Coatings, crusts and marinades create a barrier between the flesh of the fish and the surface the fish is being cooked on. I love using yogurt as a marinade for meatier fish like monkfish and pollock and it works particularly well when barbecuing. (See also the tandoori mackerel recipe on pages 10–11.) Panko breadcrumbs are excellent for crusts, but sesame seeds work equally well.

PAN-FRIED HAKE FILLET

SERVES 1

This is my preferred method for pan-frying fish. I start cooking the fillet in a pan to achieve the caramelisation and crispy skin and finish it in the oven to make sure it cooks evenly.

1 hake fillet

fine sea salt

2 tbsp vegetable oil (or any flavourless oil with a high smoke point)

Preheat the oven to 190°C (170°C fan).

Remove your fish from the fridge 15 minutes before you cook it. The fish should always be the final component of the dish to be cooked. Put it on a baking tray, pat it dry with kitchen paper to remove any excess moisture and season with fine sea salt.

Preheat your frying pan on a medium high heat for about 2 minutes. The goal here is to achieve an even temperature across the full surface area of the pan. Cold pockets will cause your fish to stick.

Add 2 tablespoons of a flavourless oil with a high smoke point to the preheated pan – I use vegetable oil. Allow the pan to come back up to temperature, as adding the oil will have caused the pan to cool slightly. This will take no more than 20 seconds, depending on how long the pan has been preheating.

Put the fish in the pan skin side down, laying the fillet down away from you to avoid oil splatters, which are inevitable due to the high water content in fish. Once the fish is in the pan, do not disturb the fillet or move the pan. Allow the crust of caramelisation to develop evenly. This will take about 4 minutes and will make removing the fillet much easier. Use a fish slice to confidently lift the fillet from the pan and put it on a clean baking tray. No matter what piece of fish you're cooking, when removing it from a pan, always lift it from the tail end of the fish. It causes less damage to the skin.

Depending on the size of the fillet you're cooking, the fish should now be at least 50% cooked through. Transfer the par-cooked fillet to the preheated oven. Cook for 2–4 minutes, depending on the size of the fish – the internal temperature should be at least 60°C. Alternatively, insert a cake tester in the thickest part of the fillet – if you feel any resistance as the cake tester enters the fish, it isn't cooked yet.

Serve immediately.

FISH SKIN

Fish skin is delicious when cooked until crisp and seasoned well. It's also extremely healthy, as it contains omega-3 fatty acids.

The skin of most fish species we have off the coast of Ireland is edible, but it's not always palatable. Whether or not the skin tastes good depends on how the fish was stored, prepared and cooked. Follow these tips for delicious, crispy skin.

1 Store your fillets skin side up and never stack portions on top of each other.

2 Remove fish from the fridge 15 minutes prior to cooking. Fish coming from a temperature below 5°C straight into a hot pan will curl as it hits the pan from the contrast in temperatures.

3 Season your fish just before cooking, as salt will begin to draw water from the fish.

4 If there is any excess moisture on the skin, pat it dry with kitchen paper before cooking.

5 Fish skin should always be scaled before it's cooked and eaten. For example, although cod skin is edible, I prefer to serve it skinned as the scales on cod are incredibly tight and tough to remove.

NOT EDIBLE	AVOID
• Bonito	• Cod
• Brill	• Halibut
• Dover sole	• Turbot
• Monkfish	
• Skate/ray	
• Tuna	

MUSSELS ESCABECHE

SERVES 4

Escabeche is a dish where the main ingredient is usually an oily fish like mackerel or shellfish (it can also be made with meat) marinated in a vinegar and olive oil solution that's been infused with herbs and spices. There are many variations of this dish in Spain, Portugal and Mexico. I love serving this dish as one of many. Leftovers are great warmed through a simple tomato sauce and served with pasta.

1kg mussels

150ml white wine

100ml olive oil

2 garlic cloves, sliced

1 bay leaf

1 lemon

2 tsp smoked paprika

50ml apple cider vinegar

Clean the mussels as per the instructions on page 28.

Put a medium-sized heavy-based pot on a medium-high heat to preheat for 3 minutes. Add the mussels, then immediately pour in the white wine. Cover the pot with a tight-fitting lid and give the pot a little shake. Cook, covered, for 3 minutes. Remove the lid – all the mussels should be cooked and open at this stage.

Drain the mussels in a large colander (reserve the stock produced for another use). Allow the mussels to cool slightly before picking the meat from the shells. Discard any mussels that haven't opened. Put the picked mussels in a small bowl and set aside.

Heat the oil in a small saucepan on a medium-low heat. Add the garlic and bay leaf and cook for 3 minutes.

WHAT IS REGENERATIVE AQUACULTURE?

Regenerative aquaculture is the rehabilitation and conservation of the ocean through farming. Seaweeds and shellfish like oysters and mussels are grown as viable food sources that require very little resources compared to agriculture.

The practice of regenerative ocean farming restores ecosystems and replenishes wild fish stocks. Oysters, mussels and shellfish improve water quality through filtration, sequester carbon and nitrogen, and provide homes and ecosystems to other marine life. These delicious molluscs and sea plants are foods that you can feel good about eating.

Using a vegetable peeler, peel two lengths of zest from the lemon and add them to the pan along with the smoked paprika. Cook for 2 minutes to infuse the oil, then add the apple cider vinegar and cook for 1 minute more. Remove the pan from the heat and discard the bay leaf and lemon zest.

Add the escabeche liquid to the mussels while it's still warm and mix well. Allow to marinate in the fridge for at least 3 hours before serving. This can be served cold, at room temperature or warmed through and will keep in the fridge for up to three days.

MUSSELS WITH CREAMED WATERCRESS & CIDER

SERVES 4

I love big bowls of juicy, plump steamed mussels, but the real star of this dish is the delightful broth created by the umami-rich sea essence released by the mussels married with the peppery creamed watercress and dry, fruity cider. This recipe also works well with clams and cockles or a mix of all three.

1kg mussels

200ml cider

FOR THE CREAMED WATERCRESS:

2 tbsp vegetable oil

1 onion, sliced

4 garlic cloves, sliced

100ml white wine

300ml cream

80g watercress

15g fresh parsley

sea salt and a pinch of ground white pepper

TO SERVE:

crusty bread

Fill a large bowl with water, then add the mussels (discard any that have cracked shells or don't close when gently tapped on the counter). Using a small paring knife, remove the beard and any barnacles from the shells. Rinse the cleaned mussels in a colander and refrigerate until just before cooking.

To make the creamed watercress, heat the oil in a large saucepan over a medium-low heat. Add the onion and garlic and cook for 5 minutes to develop their sweeter notes.

Increase the heat to medium-high. Add the white wine and cook off the alcohol until it has reduced by two-thirds. This is a crucial step – the taste of uncooked alcohol will ruin this dish. Add the cream and bring to the boil to reduce by half – this will take about 3 minutes. Remove the pan from the heat and add the watercress and parsley.

Using a hand blender, blitz on a high speed until everything has amalgamated together and is a vivid green. Taste and season with a little salt and white pepper. It's important to remember that mussels are naturally high in salt, so go easy on the salt here. You can make the creamed watercress a day ahead and add it straight from the fridge to the cooked mussels. It also freezes well for up to six weeks.

To cook the mussels, heat a heavy-based pot on a medium-high heat for 3 minutes. Drain the mussels and add them to the pot. Immediately pour in the cider and cover the pot with a tight-fitting lid. Give the pot a little shake and cook, covered, for 3 minutes.

Remove the lid – all the mussels should be cooked and open at this stage. Discard any that haven't opened. Add the creamed watercress and bring the sauce back to the boil. Taste the broth and adjust the seasoning.

Divide the mussels and the sauce among four wide, shallow bowls. Crusty bread for dipping is non-negotiable.

HOW TO
SHUCK AN OYSTER

On the island of Ireland, Pacific oysters are available all year round, while native oysters are in season in Ireland from September to April (when there's an R in the month). Both Pacific and native oysters are purified in UV-treated water before they can legally be sold. We are lucky to have oyster farms dotted around the coast of Ireland. These farms not only provide us with a delicious, nutrient-rich food source, but they also improve our water quality and provide crucial habitats for other marine life.

ESSENTIAL EQUIPMENT:
- Clean tea towel
- Oyster knife
- Small paintbrush
- Serving dish with a layer of crushed ice, fresh seaweed or coarse sea salt

1 Have your serving dish, plate or bowl ready before you start. Add a layer of crushed ice, fresh seaweed or coarse sea salt to provide a stable base to serve the oysters on. This will keep the oyster liquid and any garnish inside the oyster.

2 Fold a clean tea towel in half twice lengthways. Put the oyster in the centre of the folded towel, cup side down, with the hinge of the oyster facing in the direction of your dominant hand (i.e. the hand you write with).

3 Make sure you are shucking oysters on a flat surface. The tea towel will help protect your non-dominant hand and will keep the oyster in a stable position when the oyster is opened, limiting the loss of the glorious liquid inside the shell.

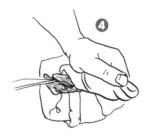

4 Place the tip of the oyster knife at the hinge of the shell, applying pressure. Now twist the knife to pop the hinge. This might require you to wiggle the knife a little, depending on the oyster. Avoid excess force, as this will shatter and chip the outside of the shell and could potentially damage the meat inside – and you!

5 Once you've popped the hinge, angle the knife towards the cup side of the shell and run your knife towards the top side of the shell. Turn the knife at a 90° angle to separate the flat side of the shell (i.e. the top shell) from the cup (i.e. the bottom shell).

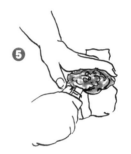

6 Use the paintbrush to remove any shell fragments that might be around the top side of the shell and the mantle of the oyster.

7 Run the knife under the oyster meat at an angle to remove the adductor muscle from the meat. Do this carefully to avoid damaging the oyster with the knife and losing any liquid.

8 Enjoy the oyster au naturel or garnish it with your favourite condiments.

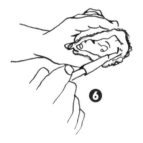

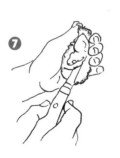

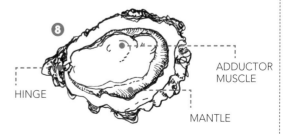

ADDUCTOR MUSCLE

HINGE

MANTLE

BAKED OYSTER & KIMCHI ROCKEFELLER

MAKES 12

Cooked oysters of any kind, be it baked, fried or poached, are a fantastic way to introduce them to anyone who is wary of eating raw shellfish. Kimchi and oysters are one of those dreamy combinations. Sweet, salty, creamy oysters work so well with the sourness and heat of kimchi. The beauty of this recipe is that everything can be prepared in advance and then popped in the oven.

coarse sea salt

12 oysters, shucked (see pages 30–31)

2 tbsp vegetable oil

65g panko breadcrumbs

FOR THE KIMCHI BUTTER:

130g unsalted butter, softened

90g kimchi, finely chopped

¼ tsp lemon zest

¼ tsp gochugaru (Korean chilli flakes)

TO SERVE:

lemon wedges

TRY THIS

If you want to make your own kimchi, try the empty-the-fridge kimchi in *Blasta Books #7: Wasted* or the West Cork kimchi in *Blasta Books #9: Funky*.

To make the kimchi butter, mix the butter, kimchi, lemon zest and the gochugaru until well combined.

Preheat the oven to 220°C (200°C fan).

Prepare a baking tray with a bed of coarse sea salt. This will provide a stable base to hold the oysters in place while they're cooking. Salt is also a great conductor of heat and won't burn or upset the flavour of the final dish.

Shuck the oysters following the instructions on pages 30–31, making sure to remove the adductor muscle and retain at least 50% of the liquid. (The amount of water inside each oyster varies according to where it was grown as well as the season.) Put the oysters on the bed of salt as you shuck them.

Put 1 tablespoon of kimchi butter in the centre of each oyster.

Heat the oil in a frying pan on a medium-low heat. Add the breadcrumbs and toast until golden brown, stirring all the time to ensure they toast evenly.

Bake the kimchi buttered oysters in the oven for 6 minutes. Remove the tray from the oven and add a heaped teaspoon of toasted panko breadcrumbs on top of each one, then return to the oven to cook for a further 2 minutes.

The oyster shells will be very hot when removed from the oven, so allow them to sit for a couple of minutes before serving with lemon wedges.

OYSTERS WITH ELDERFLOWER VINEGAR GRANITA & CHIVE OIL

MAKES 12

This is one of my favourite ways to serve oysters at Goldie. The floral, musky flavour of the elderflower vinegar works so well with the minerality of the oysters. This is my dream start to a meal on a hot summer evening.

12 oysters, shucked
(see pages 30–31)

FOR THE ELDERFLOWER VINEGAR:

10 elderflower heads

500ml unpasteurised apple cider vinegar

FOR THE ELDERFLOWER VINEGAR GRANITA:

50g caster sugar

100ml water

100ml elderflower vinegar

FOR THE CHIVE OIL:

100g fresh chives, roughly chopped

150ml vegetable oil

You'll need to make the elderflower vinegar when elderflowers are in season in June and July or see the tip on the next page. Pick them on a dry day away from any busy roadsides. Shake off any insects on the flower heads but do not wash the flowers. Put the elderflower heads in a sterile 500ml jar and pour over the apple cider vinegar. Give the jar a good shake and leave in a cool, dark place for a least one month to infuse. We use this exact same process for lemon verbena when we get gluts of it during the summer and serve that with our oysters too.

To make the granita, warm the sugar and water in a small saucepan on a medium-low heat. When the sugar has dissolved, remove the pan from the heat and stir in the elderflower vinegar. Allow to cool to room temperature, then transfer to a shallow container. Put in a freezer for 2 hours, until completely frozen.

To make the chive oil, put the chives and vegetable oil in a food processor and blend on full speed until the chives resemble a paste and the oil starts to take on the colour of the chives.

Transfer the chive pulp and oil from the food processor to a small saucepan. Cook on a medium-high heat until the mixture hits 86°C. At this temperature, the chive pulp will have transferred its flavour and colour to the oil.

Take the pan off the heat. Pass the oil through a fine mesh sieve lined with cheesecloth or a coffee filter. Discard the pulp and allow the oil to cool before transferring it to a

clean jar and storing in the fridge for up to a week, at which point it will begin to lose its colour and flavour. Alternatively, you can freeze it in an ice cube tray, then pop the cubes into a freezerproof bag and store in the freezer for up to three months.

To serve, scratch the surface of the granita with a spoon to produce little ice crystals. Add a heaped teaspoon of granita to each shucked oyster and drizzle with a little chive oil.

TRY THIS

If elderflowers are out of season, you could add a little elderflower cordial to the apple cider vinegar instead and reduce the amount of sugar used in the granita to compensate for the sugar in the cordial.

CRAB MADAME

MAKES 4

A huge part of what we do at Goldie is preparing menu items that are familiar to everyone. As a seafood restaurant, we are aware of our limitations when it comes to what we can offer our guests. We want to appeal to lovers of food, not just lovers of fish. This crab madame – the queen of sandwiches – is a fantastic example of that.

As a rule of thumb, I don't like to serve fish with cheese. I'm not convinced of the combination. However, there are exceptions, especially for shellfish. The cheese in this recipe reinforces the sweetness of the crab. Picking brown crab meat is a laborious task for us at the restaurant, but luckily, cooked and picked shell-free crab meat can be easily purchased.

500g crab meat, picked

2 tbsp chopped fresh parsley

2 tbsp Dijon mustard

¼ tsp lemon zest

sea salt and freshly ground black pepper

8 slices of white yeast bread

40g salted butter, melted

1 tbsp vegetable oil

100g cheese, grated (I use Cáis na Tíre)

4 eggs

FOR THE BÉCHAMEL SAUCE:

500ml milk

½ onion, sliced

1 garlic clove, crushed

1 bay leaf

5 black peppercorns

75g unsalted butter

75g plain flour

First, make the béchamel sauce. Warm the milk, onion, garlic, bay leaf and black peppercorns in a small saucepan over a medium-low heat for 10 minutes. Remove the onion, garlic, bay leaf and peppercorns.

Melt the butter in a separate heavy-based, medium-sized saucepan on a medium heat, then add the flour and stir well using a wooden spoon. Cook for 2 minutes before adding the warmed milk slowly and gradually to prevent lumps forming in the sauce. Once all the milk has been added, reduce the heat to low and cook for a further 5 minutes to ensure the flour is cooked.

Pour the sauce into a medium-sized mixing bowl, then press some greaseproof paper directly on top of the surface to prevent a skin forming. Allow to cool, then remove 100g of the béchamel and set it aside for the topping.

Preheat the oven to 190°C (170°C fan).

Add the picked crab meat, parsley, mustard and lemon zest to the béchamel sauce and mix well. Taste and season with salt and freshly cracked black pepper. >>

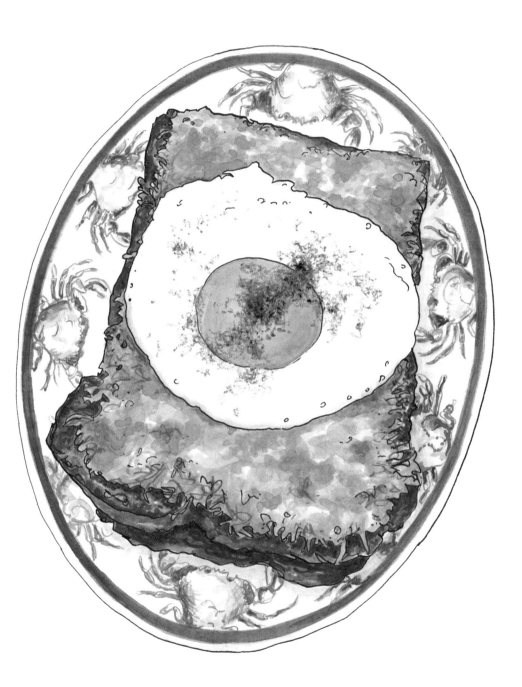

TO GARNISH:

nori powder

Lay out four slices of bread. Spread 150g of the crab béchamel filling on each slice before sandwiching with the other slices. Brush the top of each sandwich with the melted salted butter.

Heat the oil in a large frying pan on a medium heat. Working in batches, put the sandwiches in the pan with the buttered sides facing down and cook until nicely toasted. Brush the tops of the sandwiches with melted butter, then carefully flip the sandwiches over to toast the other side too.

Put the four toasted sandwiches on a baking tray. Spread the top of each sandwich with 25g of the reserved béchamel before adding 25g of grated cheese on top of each one. Bake in the preheated oven for 12 minutes, until the filling is piping hot and the béchamel and cheese topping are golden brown.

While the crab madames are in the oven, fry the eggs sunny side up. Serve one fried egg on top of each sandwich with a sprinkle of sea salt and nori powder.

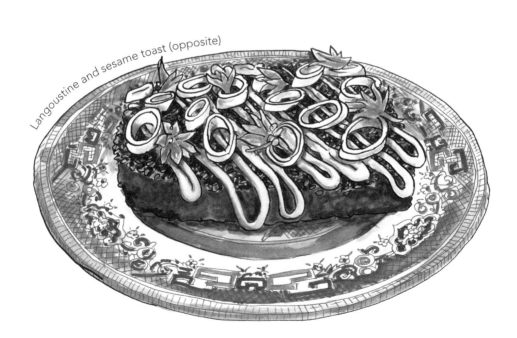

Langoustine and sesame toast (opposite)

LANGOUSTINE & SESAME TOAST

MAKES 4

This is such a simple yet rewarding recipe. The nuttiness of sesame works so well with sweet langoustines and the sesame seed coating acts as a non-stick barrier in the pan. A small quantity of precious langoustines goes a long way in this recipe. When we do this at Goldie, we make shokupan, a Japanese milk bread, and serve the toast with a salted lemon mayonnaise.

365g langoustine tails

1 garlic clove, grated

1 tsp grated fresh ginger

1 tsp toasted sesame oil

½ tsp fine sea salt

a pinch of ground white pepper

3 spring onions

45g black sesame seeds

45g white sesame seeds

4 x 1cm-thick slices of white yeast bread, crusts on

4 tbsp vegetable oil

Japanese mayonnaise or salted lemon mayo (page 61), to serve

Remove the langoustine heads and shells from the tails (keep them for stock – see the recipe on page 40). Using a sharp knife, make a small incision down the centre of each langoustine tail to remove the intestinal tract.

Using a sharp chef's knife, finely chop the langoustines until they form a paste. Put the paste in a mixing bowl with the garlic, ginger, toasted sesame oil, salt and white pepper. Mix well.

Finely chop the green tops of the spring onions, add them to the bowl and mix to combine. Thinly slice the white parts at an angle and set aside.

Combine the black and white sesame seeds and put them on a small tray or plate.

Using a butter knife or an offset spatula, spread 1 tablespoon of the seasoned langoustine paste on one side of a slice of bread, then dip the bread in the sesame seeds to coat the paste. Do the same on the other side of the bread. Repeat with the rest of the paste and bread.

Heat the oil in a large frying pan on a medium heat. Working in batches so that you don't crowd the pan, add the toasts and cook for 4 minutes on each side, until golden brown. Remove from the pan and drain on kitchen paper.

To serve, drizzle each slice with Japanese or salted lemon mayonnaise, then scatter over the sliced spring onions.

LANGOUSTINE SCAMPI WITH KATSU CURRY SAUCE

SERVES 4

Langoustines are my favourite crustacean, not only for their sweet and succulent tails, but for the bountiful flavour provided in the heads and shells. We use 100% of the langoustine in the restaurant – a rarity when handling over 150kg of whole fish and shellfish each week. This recipe is a homage to scampi, chips and curry sauce.

1.5kg langoustines (approx. 45 langoustines)

85g plain flour

1 egg

200ml milk

150g panko breadcrumbs

vegetable oil, for deep-frying

FOR THE KATSU CURRY SAUCE:

60g vegetable oil

60g butter

1 onion, sliced

8 garlic cloves, sliced

70g ginger, peeled and diced

a pinch of fine sea salt

4 tsp curry powder

500ml coconut milk

2 tbsp ketchup

1 tbsp Worcestershire sauce

Preheat the oven to 180°C (160°C fan).

To prepare the langoustines, remove the heads and shells from the tails (keep them for the stock). Using a sharp knife, make a small incision down the centre of each langoustine tail to remove the intestinal tract.

Put the tails in a single layer on a baking tray or plate and refrigerate for 30 minutes before breadcrumbing. Once shelled, langoustines are extremely perishable.

Meanwhile, to make the langoustine stock, put 500g of the heads and shells in a small roasting tin and toss with the oil. Roast in the preheated oven for 25 minutes. Remove from the oven and put all the roasted heads and shells into a pot. Scrape the tray to remove any sediment and get that into the pot too. Cover with 2 litres of cold water and bring to the boil, then reduce the heat to medium-low and simmer for 30 minutes. This makes 2 litres of stock but you need only 500ml for this recipe, so set that aside and freeze the rest for soups and sauces – it will keep in the freezer for up to eight weeks.

To make the katsu curry sauce, heat the oil and butter in a heavy-based pot on a medium-low heat. Add the onion, garlic and ginger and season with sea salt. Cook for 15 minutes, until golden.

Add the curry powder and cook for 2 minutes to bloom the spices. Add the 500ml of langoustine stock, then give the bottom of the pot a good scrape with a wooden

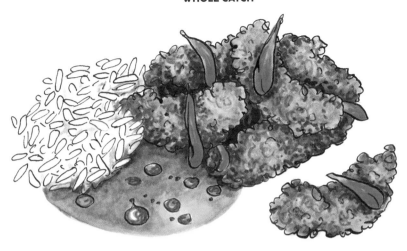

FOR THE STOCK:

500g langoustine heads and tails

1 tbsp vegetable oil

2 litres cold water

TO SERVE:

boiled rice

spoon to get all that flavour into the sauce. Stir in the coconut milk and simmer for 20 minutes, until the sauce has reduced and coats the back of a wooden spoon.

Add the ketchup and Worcestershire to the sauce, then blitz it with a hand blender and pass through a fine mesh sieve. Keep warm.

To crumb the langoustines, put the flour in a wide, shallow bowl. Beat the egg with the milk in a second wide, shallow bowl. Put the breadcrumbs in a third wide, shallow bowl.

Working in batches of five at a time, toss the langoustines through the flour first, then through the milk and egg mixture, and finally through the panko breadcrumbs, shaking off the excess flour, egg and milk, and breadcrumbs at each stage. Put the breaded langoustines on a baking tray or plate in the refrigerator until ready to cook – you can do this ahead of time or even the day before.

Heat the oil in a deep-fryer to 180°C.

Working in batches, fry the breaded langoustines for 2 minutes, until golden brown. Drain on kitchen paper and season with sea salt.

Serve with the katsu curry sauce and some boiled rice.

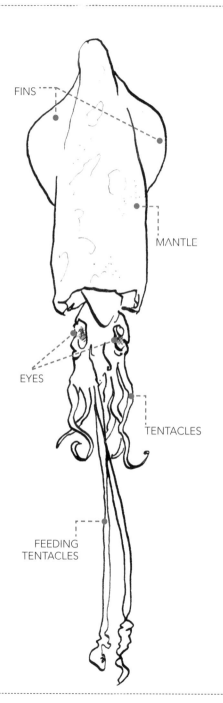

FINS

MANTLE

EYES

TENTACLES

FEEDING
TENTACLES

HOW TO
PREPARE
A SQUID

Squid needs to cook either quickly, like in the calamari on page 44, or slowly, like in the dal on page 46, to avoid it becoming rubbery.

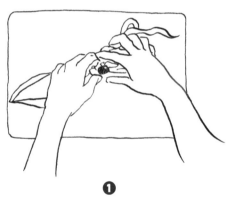

1

To prepare a squid, pull the tentacles away from the main body, gripping it with your thumb and forefinger just above the eyes. Discard the internal organs attached but reserve the ink sac to use in the braised squid with beluga lentil dal on page 46, in a risotto or in the squid ink and stout battered hake in *Blasta Books #2: Hot Fat.*

2

Remove the quill (a hard, flat piece of cartilage that resembles a piece of plastic) from inside the mantle of the squid.

3

Detach the wing-like fins by carefully pulling them away from the torso, removing the purple outer membrane of the squid at the same time.

3

4

Cut directly beneath the eye to remove the tentacles from the internal organs and discard the beak.

5

Trim the longer feeding tentacles to the same length as the other tentacles.

6

Peel away the outer membrane from the tentacles.

7

Cut the mantle of the squid into 1cm-thick rings and put them in a colander. Rinse to remove any lingering innards, drain well and refrigerate along with the tentacles until just before cooking.

CALAMARI WITH VIETNAMESE CHILLI SAUCE

SERVES 4

Calamari is one of my favourite seafood dishes and it's a real crowd pleaser too. This Vietnamese chilli sauce works so well with fried foods, but it's also excellent with vegetables. When squid is available, this is always my go-to dish. I love serving it with a fresh herb and onion salad dressed in some of the chilli sauce and a little extra fresh lime juice.

500g squid, prepared as per pages 42–43

vegetable oil, for deep-frying

200g potato starch

80g cornflour

40g rice flour

1 tsp baking powder

1 tsp fine sea salt

FOR THE VIETNAMESE CHILLI SAUCE:

300g caster sugar

100ml water

75ml fish sauce

3 garlic cloves, grated

3 fresh red chillies, finely chopped

juice of 3 limes

1 tsp rice wine vinegar

TO GARNISH:

thinly sliced red chilli rings

thinly sliced spring onion rings

thinly sliced red onion rings

fresh coriander leaves

To make the Vietnamese chilli sauce, put the sugar and water in a small saucepan on a medium-high heat. Bring to the boil to dissolve the sugar, then stir in the fish sauce and remove the pan from the heat. Add the garlic, chilli, lime juice and vinegar. Taste and adjust the seasoning – the sauce may need another squeeze of citrus depending on how juicy your limes are. Allow to cool before serving. This sauce keeps well in a sealed jar in the fridge for up to two weeks.

To cook the squid, heat the oil in a deep-fryer to 190°C.

Combine the potato starch, cornflour, rice flour, baking powder and salt in a bowl. Toss the sliced squid rings and tentacles through the flour mixture, making sure all the surface area of the squid is covered. Shake off any excess.

Working in batches so you don't overcrowd the fryer, which will reduce the temperature of the oil, fry the coated squid for 1 minute. Drain on kitchen paper and season with sea salt.

Garnish the calamari with thinly sliced chilli, spring onion and red onion rings and fresh coriander leaves. Serve with a small bowl of the Vietnamese chilli sauce on the side for dipping.

BRAISED SQUID WITH BELUGA LENTIL DAL

SERVES 4

Braised squid of any kind is a great way to include seafood in your diet. Here, the braising liquid from the squid is used to cook the beluga lentils. This is a great recipe to make ahead of time as it reheats and freezes well.

FOR THE SQUID:

700g whole squid

1 onion, sliced

2 garlic cloves, crushed

1 tsp coriander seeds

FOR THE DAL:

5 tbsp vegetable oil

1 tsp ground cumin

1 tsp ground coriander

½ tsp ground fenugreek

1 onion, diced

4 garlic cloves, sliced

a thumb-sized piece of ginger, peeled and finely chopped

300g beluga lentils

1 x 400ml tin of coconut milk

fine sea salt and freshly ground black pepper

1 bunch of fresh coriander, leaves picked and stems finely chopped

TO SERVE:

2 tbsp lime pickle

Prepare the squid as outlined on pages 42–43 **but skip the slicing part of step 7** – you want to keep the mantle whole. Don't forget to keep the ink sac.

Put the squid mantle and tentacles in a medium-sized heavy-based pot along with the onion, garlic and coriander seeds. Top up with cold water and bring to the boil, then reduce the heat and simmer for 30 minutes, until the squid is tender.

Remove the squid from the braising liquid, then strain the liquid through a fine mesh sieve to be used in the dal.

To make the dal, heat 3 tablespoons of oil in a medium-sized saucepan on a medium-high heat. Add the ground spices and cook for just 1 minute to extract their flavour, then add the onion, garlic and ginger and cook for 10 minutes.

Add the lentils, coconut milk, 1 litre of the strained braising liquid and the reserved ink sac from the squid. Reduce the heat to medium-low and cook, stirring regularly, for 20 minutes, until the lentils are tender. Season with salt and pepper and add more of the squid braising liquid if you feel the dal is too thick.

Cut the squid mantle into 2cm-thick rings and cut the tentacles in half lengthways. Heat the remaining 2 tablespoons of oil in a frying pan on a medium-high heat. Add the squid and sear for a couple of minutes, until golden brown.

Add the seared squid to the dal to warm through, followed by the fresh coriander, but reserve a few of the picked leaves for garnish. I love to serve this with a lime pickle.

DRY CURE

MAKES 150G

This dry cure can be used for almost any fish but it works particularly well with flat and round fish such as turbot, brill, plaice, pollock, cod and haddock. You can add spices, herbs, sake or citrus zest to this cure mix too (see the suggestions in the box). Choose extremely fresh fish for this, as the cured fish won't be cooked.

100g fine sea salt

50g caster sugar

Combine the salt and sugar in a clean, dry bowl and mix well. This lasts indefinitely and can be left in your larder to use as it suits.

Skin your fish to allow the cure to permeate the flesh. Lay the fillets flat on a deep stainless steel tray or in a glass dish, making sure they're not touching each other.

For every 5g of fish, use 1g of the dry cure (this applies to both flat and round fish). For example:

- For 100g of fish, use 20g of the dry cure.
- For 150g of fish, use 30g of the dry cure.
- For 200g of fish, use 40g of the dry cure.

Sprinkle the dry cure liberally over the fillets to coat as much surface area of the fish as possible.

Put the coated fish in the fridge, turning occasionally to ensure the fish cures evenly. For a flat fish, leave it in the cure for 2– 2½ hours. For a round fish, leave it for 3–3½ hours.

Rinse off the cure and pat the fish dry using a clean lint-free tea towel or kitchen paper. Put the fish back in the fridge to dry out, uncovered, for a couple of hours. After this time, cover the fish. The fish will now keep for up to three days.

Cut the fish into slices with a sharp knife. It can now be served any number of ways. We cover this cured fish with pastrami spice before slicing and serve it with sauerkraut and pickled mustard seeds; we serve it with freshly grated Irish wasabi; or sometimes we serve it with blood orange kosho (page 64), black rice vinegar, fresh mint and extra virgin olive oil.

RED MULLET 'ANCHOVIES'

MAKES 300G

Red mullet is one my favourite species to work with – there are endless creative opportunities with this gorgeous little apricot-coloured fish. Red mullet has a distinct flavour due to its diet and its fat content – this little sea pig loves to snack on crustaceans. The bones and head are my favourite for fish stock and sauces. This recipe preserves the fish for weeks.

6 red mullet fillets
(approx. 350g)

120g flaky sea salt

15g fresh flat-leaf parsley,
finely chopped

zest of 1 lemon

olive oil (enough to cover)

If preparing from whole, you will need to fin and scale the fish. You won't find many fish with larger or tougher scales than red mullet. Other than the scaling, the filleting process is the same as for mackerel on pages 8–9. Trim the fillets of any excess remains of the gutting/filleting process. There's no need to pin bone at this stage, as this happens after the curing process, causing less damage to the flesh.

Combine the salt, parsley and lemon zest, then sprinkle the base of a glass or non-reactive stainless steel dish with this curing mixture. Lay each fillet flesh side down in the curing mixture, ensuring there is enough of the cure on the base to cover the surface area of each fillet. Use the rest of the cure mixture to cover the skin side of the fillets.

Cover and refrigerate for three days. During this time, the salt will draw out the water from the fillets, which is necessary to preserve the fish.

After the three days, remove the fillets from the cure and rinse well to remove the excess salt, then pat dry using a lint-free tea towel or some kitchen paper. Pull the tough skin off the fish, working from the head to the tail of each fillet. Pin bone the fillets.

Transfer the fish to a sterilised glass jar or container and cover with olive oil, then seal the jar or container and refrigerate. I like to leave the fillets in the oil for at least three days before serving – the texture of the 'anchovies' benefits greatly from this.

To serve, remove the red mullet 'anchovies' from the olive oil and slice thinly. Serve the 'anchovies' simply as they are, add them to salads or sauces or use them to make your own gildas.

FRIED BOQUERONES WITH AGRODOLCE KETCHUP

SERVES 2 AS A SNACK

Boquerones are anchovies that have been filleted and marinated in vinegar, extra virgin olive oil, garlic and herbs. These are much more delicate in flavour than salted anchovies and are one of my favourite conservas, as I am a vinegar fiend. This simple recipe works so well as a quick snack before dinner or as one of a series of small plates. It also satisfies a fish 'n' chips craving without having to leave the house. Cooking these marinated little fish in a thin, crispy batter gives you all the comfort of a salt- and malt vinegar-seasoned piece of battered fish with a little European sophistication.

80g boquerones, drained

vegetable oil, for deep-frying

85g plain flour

150ml sparkling water

fine sea salt

agrodolce ketchup (page 63), to serve

Remove the boquerones from their packaging and drain off the excess olive oil and vinegar marinade.

Heat the oil in a deep-fryer to 180°C (or see the note on page 20 if you don't have a deep-fryer).

To make the batter, put 70g of the plain flour in a small mixing bowl. Make a well in the centre of the bowl and slowly add the sparkling water, whisking all the time to achieve a lump-free batter. Add a pinch of salt and set aside.

Put the remaining 15g of flour on a small plate or tray. Working with one at a time, dust the boquerones in the flour until fully coated – this step ensures that the batter will stick to the marinated anchovies. Shake off the excess flour, then add the boquerones to the batter.

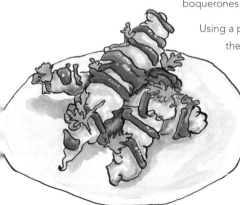

Using a pair of small kitchen tongs or a fork, delicately fetch the anchovies from the batter. Working in batches, carefully add them to the hot oil. Fry for 1 minute, until the batter is golden brown and crisp.

Drain on kitchen paper to remove any excess oil and season with sea salt. Serve immediately with agrodolce ketchup.

SHAOXING SOUSED MACKEREL

SERVES 4

Sousing is a fantastic way to prepare and serve oily fish like herring, mackerel, red mullet and sardines. The Shaoxing wine here adds a great savouriness to the marinade, which can typically be heavy on the vinegar.

2 whole mackerel (or 4 fillets)

1 tsp Szechuan peppercorns

100ml rice wine vinegar

75ml Shaoxing wine

25g caster sugar

vegetable oil, for brushing

fine sea salt

TO SERVE:

chilli oil

sliced raw vegetables or your favourite pickle

If you're preparing whole mackerel, follow the instructions on pages 8–9 **but do not pin bone the fillets**. Instead, cut the fillets in half lengthways to remove the bones. Using the bones as a guide, slice the fish away from the bones on either side of the fillet, leaving you with two long, thin mackerel fillets free from any bones. Cut these thin fillets in half widthways and put them in a deep glass or non-reactive tray, flesh side down. Set aside.

To make the marinade, first toast the Szechuan peppercorns in a hot, dry saucepan until fragrant. Add the rice wine vinegar, Shaoxing wine and sugar. Set aside.

Brush the mackerel skin with some vegetable oil and season with a little sea salt. Blowtorch the fillets until they are nicely charred but not black. If you don't have a blowtorch, put the fillets under a hot grill for a couple of minutes.

Bring the marinade to the boil in the saucepan, then pass it through a fine mesh sieve to remove the peppercorns, pouring it directly over the charred mackerel. Leave to marinate for 20 minutes, until the mackerel has cooled.

This will keep for up to three days in the fridge. I like to serve this warm, but it can also be enjoyed cold. Serve with your favourite chilli oil, some freshly sliced raw vegetables, like courgette or carrot, or your favourite pickles.

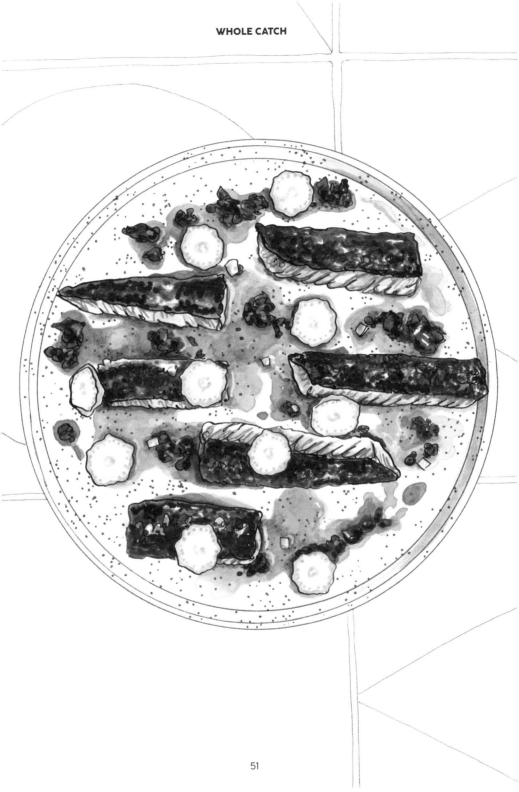

SMOKED MACKEREL PÂTÉ

MAKES 250G

There is something comforting about smoked fish and this pâté is one of my favourite seafood dishes. Serve it as a starter with crackers or crusty bread and lots of pickles, as a focal point of a salad or as a scrumptious sandwich filler.

1 whole smoked mackerel or
2 smoked mackerel fillets

100g mayonnaise

60g crème fraîche

zest and juice of 1 lemon

2 tbsp chopped fresh parsley

1 tbsp chopped fresh dill

½ tsp fine sea salt

½ tsp freshly ground black pepper

If using a whole smoked mackerel, put it on a chopping board with the cavity of the fish facing you. Detach the head and pull, working from the head down to the tail, to remove the main frame of the fish at the same time. Separate the two fillets.

Whether or not you're using the whole mackerel or two smoked fillets, slowly flake the fish away from the skin. Do so carefully to avoid bones. Put the picked flakes of mackerel in a small mixing bowl and set aside.

Put the mayonnaise, crème fraîche, lemon zest and juice and chopped herbs in a separate bowl. Mix well to combine, then add the flaked mackerel and fold it through. It's important not to overmix at this point, as you want to have nice chunky flakes of smoked mackerel running through the pâté. Add the salt and pepper, then adjust the seasoning to taste.

This pâté keeps in the fridge for up to three days and can be made in advance.

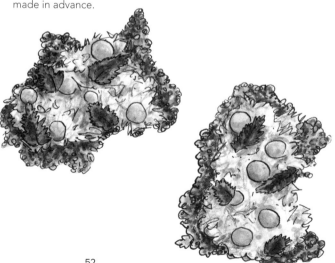

TRY THIS

You can also use canned tuna, mackerel or trout here – you need 150g of drained fish for this recipe.

SALT FISH, CHICKPEA & TOMATO SALAD

SERVES 2

Salt fish is such a versatile ingredient to have in your fridge (see the recipe intro on the next page if you'd like to have a go at making it yourself). The stable shelf life is a great bonus but being organised enough to soak the fish properly is essential to this quick little dish. I'm using chickpeas here, but you could use just about any pulse you have at home.

150g salt fish

4 tbsp olive oil

2 garlic cloves, sliced

1 x 400g tin of chickpeas, drained and rinsed

fine sea salt and freshly ground black pepper

8 ripe cherry tomatoes, halved

1 small red onion, sliced

1 bunch of fresh parsley, chopped

juice of 1 lemon

Rinse the salt fish to remove any excess salt on the exterior. Soak the rinsed fish in 600ml of cold water overnight, changing the water twice. This allows the fish to rehydrate and removes extra salt.

The next day, preheat the oven to 180°C (160°C fan). Drain the fish.

Put the soaked and drained salt fish on a baking tray and coat with 2 tablespoons of the oil. Bake in the preheated oven for 8 minutes, until a cake tester glides through the flesh with no resistance. Remove from the oven and flake the fish into a small bowl.

While the fish is baking, heat the remaining 2 tablespoons of oil in a small saucepan on a medium-low heat. Add the garlic and cook for 5 minutes, being careful that the garlic doesn't catch. Add the chickpeas and season with salt and pepper, then remove the pan from the heat.

Add the cooked, flaked salt fish along with the tomatoes, onion, parsley and lemon juice. Toss gently to combine, then divide between two plates.

You can serve this salad hot, cold or at room temperature.

SALT FISH BRANDADE

MAKES 850G

Brandade has featured on our menu in one way or another since Goldie opened in 2019. It's versatile, delicious and a fantastic use of trim. Salting is one of our most-used methods for preserving gluts and leftovers. You can buy salt fish at most fishmongers, but it's satisfying and practical to make your own. Just put a layer of salt in the base of a non-reactive dish, followed by the fresh fish, then cover in another layer of salt. After a day or two, most of the water will have been removed from the fish. Remove the fish from the water-saturated salt and repeat the process of layering with salt in a clean, dry container, then cover with a tight-fitting lid and refrigerate. This will preserve the fish, so it can be stored like this for months. It can then be added to pasta dishes, sauces, soups, croquettes and fish cakes.

250g salt fish

2 tbsp vegetable oil

1 onion, sliced

4 garlic cloves, sliced

150ml white wine

550g potato, peeled and diced

300ml water

4 tbsp extra virgin olive oil

sea salt and freshly ground black pepper

Rinse the salt fish to remove any excess salt on the exterior. Soak the rinsed fish in 600ml of cold water overnight, changing the water once. This allows the fish to rehydrate and it also removes extra salt.

The next day, drain the fish. Heat the vegetable oil in a medium-sized saucepan on a medium-low heat. Add the onion and garlic and cook for about 15 minutes, until soft and sweet.

Increase the heat to medium-high and add the wine. Bring to the boil and reduce until the wine has completely evaporated. This is important, as the taste of raw wine will ruin this dish.

Add the diced potato and salt fish and top up with the water. Bring to the boil and pop a lid on the pan, then reduce the heat and simmer for about 15 minutes, until the potato is just cooked. Remove the lid and bring to the boil to evaporate the water, stirring all the time to prevent catching.

Emulsify the contents of the pot with a hand blender. Add the olive oil, then taste and season. Depending on the salt fish, the brandade may require a little more salt.

Put some greaseproof paper directly over the brandade as it cools to prevent a skin from forming. Transfer to an airtight container covered with a lid and store in the fridge, where it will keep for up to three days.

Serve at room temperature or warm, but never cold. Serve as a snack with pickles (it would be especially good with the pickled sea kale, garlic scapers, pickled green beans or pickled fennel in *Blasta Books #9: Funky*) and crackers or use as a base for a summer salad. I love serving brandade with sweet summer tomatoes, thinly sliced courgettes and a crusty baguette.

CANNED FISH IS FRESH FISH

Glistening fresh fish is not always easily accessible depending on your location, how often you can get to the fishmonger, farmers market or supermarket, how much refrigeration space you have at home and, of course, the weather. Canned fish should not be seen as an alternative to fresh fish – canned fish *is* fresh fish. Canned fish is often processed and preserved within hours of landing, at the peak of its freshness and with little waste.

There are many perks to canned fish. It doesn't need to be refrigerated, it doesn't use plastic and it's usually labelled well. Labelling is an area within the seafood industry that requires massive improvement and legislative reform. Clearly displayed fishing methods and locations are a huge benefit. Look for the terms 'line caught' or 'pole caught'. These fishing methods eliminate bycatch, which in turn promotes the wellbeing of other species. We should all keep sustainability in mind when buying fish or fish products. It's important to consider not just the species, but also how it was caught, where it was caught and how that fishery is managed. I know this seems like a daunting task before you even start cooking, but the future of our oceans deserves this consideration.

The possibilities of canned fish go far beyond one of my favourite ways to use it, in tuna and mayonnaise sandwiches. Think classic Caesar and Niçoise salads, dips, spreads and pâtés, pasta dishes, toasts and fish cakes. Canned shellfish, mussels, clams and cockles provide dinner in a matter of moments.

Here are three of my favourite ways to use canned fish:

1 Add a couple nests of noodles and a can of tinned mussels or clams to some miso soup for a quick ramen dinner.

2 Sri Lankan fish cutlets – a breaded croquette – are a popular snack. Sweat an onion with some garlic, ginger, green chilli and curry powder. Cool and add to a mixing bowl with a tin of mackerel and some cooked, cooled potatoes. Shape into balls and coat in breadcrumbs before deep-frying. Serve with the Goldie house hot sauce on page 65.

3 Set up a tinned fish and pickles board instead of a meat and cheese board.

TONNATO DRESSING

MAKES 400G

Tonnato is a thick, creamy, mayonnaise-based sauce made by blending tuna with olive oil and a few more ingredients. This sauce comes from Piedmont, Italy, where it's served with thin slices of cold veal. I love serving it with some freshly picked salad leaves and briny capers – to be honest, you need very little else. I like to make this emulsion a little looser than it's typically made so that it generously coats lettuce leaves. It also works incredibly well with leftover roast chicken.

110g tinned tuna

2 egg yolks, at room temperature

2 anchovy fillets

1 garlic clove, grated

juice of 1 lemon

200ml vegetable oil

2 tbsp extra virgin olive oil

50ml water

½ tsp freshly cracked black pepper

Drain the tuna from the oil it may be in, but don't discard the oil – measure it and use whatever amount you have to make up the 200ml of vegetable oil. This still applies even if the tuna has been tinned in olive oil, as lighter varieties are used in the canning process.

Put the drained tuna, egg yolks, anchovy fillets, grated garlic and lemon juice in a small bowl. Using a hand blender, purée all the ingredients until smooth. Alternatively, you can do this in a food processor.

Put the vegetable oil and extra virgin olive oil in a small jug. Slowly whisk the oils into the tuna and egg yolk mixture until thick and emulsified. Add the water to loosen this mixture, keeping in mind that you want something thick and creamy but also pourable. Add the cracked black pepper, then taste and adjust the seasoning as needed.

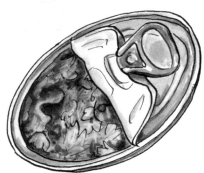

TARAMASALATA

MAKES 275G

Taramasalata is a Greek dish of smoked fish roe (usually of cod or mullet) that's emulsified with olive oil. It's smoky, creamy, delicately fishy and delicious. It can be made with pretty much any fish roe. We have hot smoked and used the roe of plaice, cod, turbot and John Dory when making this sauce at Goldie. You can buy smoked fish roe online or in speciality delis. Cod roe is the most widely available. The roe keeps well in the freezer for months. I love serving this with raw, brined or pickled vegetables and crusty bread. In the illustration, it's served with salt-brined baby turnips and their tops.

100g hot smoked John Dory roe (or see the intro), removed from the sac

juice of ½ lemon

100ml extra virgin olive oil

75ml vegetable oil

a pinch of salt

Slice through the smoked roe to reveal the eggs inside. Scoop out the eggs and discard the outer sac membrane.

Put the smoked fish eggs in a small bowl with the lemon juice and blend using a hand blender. The eggs will begin to break down a little and become paler.

Put the extra virgin olive oil in a small jug and slowly add this to the smoked roe and lemon juice while blending. Once emulsified, repeat with the vegetable oil.

When both oils have been added, you'll have a thick, creamy sauce. Season with a pinch of salt and add more lemon juice if necessary. Smoked roe is salted or brined prior to smoking, so it's important to taste the sauce before adding any extra seasoning. Store in the fridge until serving. This sauce keeps for three days, so it can be made ahead of time.

CAFÉ DE PARIS BUTTER

MAKES 500G

This compound butter sauce originated in Geneva and is most often served with steak. However, it also works incredibly well with so many fish species that we have off the island of Ireland – it's a sauce that almost never comes off the menu in Goldie. This butter keeps well for a week in the fridge and can be frozen too. I spread it on toast, slather it on new potatoes and add a couple of knobs to steamed greens.

450g salted butter, diced and softened

1 small onion, roughly chopped

2 garlic cloves, roughly chopped

2 anchovy fillets, roughly chopped

80g gherkins, roughly chopped

1 bunch of fresh flat-leaf parsley, stems and leaves roughly chopped

zest and juice of 1 lemon

1 tbsp ketchup

1 tbsp Dijon mustard

1 tbsp Worcestershire sauce

2 tsp capers

1 tsp curry powder

½ tsp smoked paprika

¼ tsp ground black pepper

a pinch of cayenne pepper

Remove the butter from the fridge a couple of hours before you make this recipe.

Put all the ingredients except the butter in a food processor and blend into a smooth purée.

Put the diced butter in a stand mixer fitted with the paddle attachment and beat on a medium speed until it's light and smooth. Scrape down the sides of the bowl and add half of the purée, then beat on a low speed before adding the rest. Initially the mixture will look split but keep mixing and scraping down the sides of the bowl and it will all come together.

Working in batches, shape the Café de Paris butter into logs on parchment paper using a spatula. Roll these up tightly, twisting the ends like a Christmas cracker to seal, and store in the fridge or freezer.

To serve, you can add a couple of slices over a just-baked, grilled or steamed piece of fish. I prefer to gently melt a couple of tablespoons on a low heat and spoon the melted butter onto the plate to ensure maximum surface area saucing.

MAYONNAISE X 3

MAKES 600ML

Serve this mayonnaise with any fried fish or scampi or add a couple of tablespoons to some hot smoked mackerel with a little diced fresh chilli for a delicious sandwich filling.

2 limes (for lime or togarashi mayo) or 2 lemons (for salted lemon mayo)

3 egg yolks, at room temperature

a pinch of fine sea salt

500ml vegetable oil

1 LIME MAYO

I make emulsions in a stand mixer fitted with a whisk attachment, as you can slowly add the oil with far less chance of splitting the sauce. Alternatively, you can use a food processor or a hand-held electric whisk with a mixing bowl set on a tea towel.

Zest and juice the limes. Put the egg yolks, lime zest and juice and a pinch of salt in a large, spotlessly clean mixing bowl or the bowl of your stand mixer. Whisk well for 1 minute.

Using a measuring jug, slowly add the vegetable oil a few drops at a time, whisking until the mixture is fully combined before adding any more oil. Patience at the beginning of this process is essential, so take your time. As you continue to slowly add more of the oil, the emulsion will become stronger and you'll be able to add more oil at a time.

Once all the oil has been added and you have a thick, homogenous sauce, taste and adjust the seasoning, adding more lime juice and salt if needed. This will keep in a sealed jar in the fridge for three days.

2 TOGARASHI MAYO

Togarashi is a Japanese spice mix that is also called Japanese seven spice. It's made of various seeds, chillies, citrus zest and seaweed. To make a togarashi mayo to serve with the karaage hake nuggets on page 19, use lime juice (no zest) and add a pinch of sugar along with the salt, then proceed as in the lime mayo recipe. Stir in 2 teaspoons of togarashi at the very end, once the mayo has emulsified.

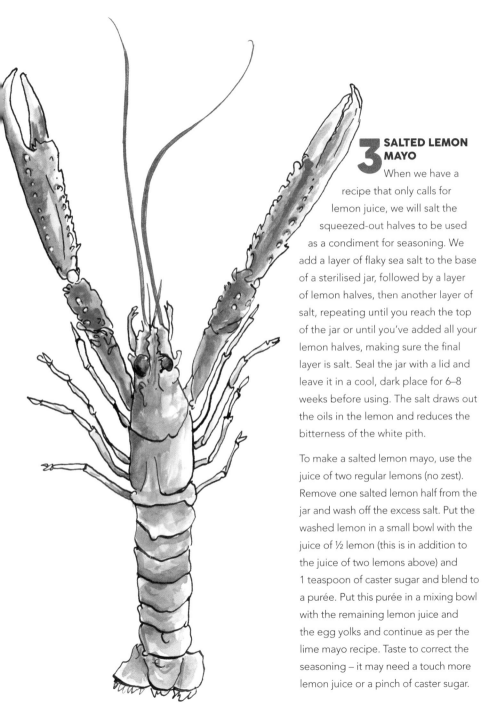

3 SALTED LEMON MAYO

When we have a recipe that only calls for lemon juice, we will salt the squeezed-out halves to be used as a condiment for seasoning. We add a layer of flaky sea salt to the base of a sterilised jar, followed by a layer of lemon halves, then another layer of salt, repeating until you reach the top of the jar or until you've added all your lemon halves, making sure the final layer is salt. Seal the jar with a lid and leave it in a cool, dark place for 6–8 weeks before using. The salt draws out the oils in the lemon and reduces the bitterness of the white pith.

To make a salted lemon mayo, use the juice of two regular lemons (no zest). Remove one salted lemon half from the jar and wash off the excess salt. Put the washed lemon in a small bowl with the juice of ½ lemon (this is in addition to the juice of two lemons above) and 1 teaspoon of caster sugar and blend to a purée. Put this purée in a mixing bowl with the remaining lemon juice and the egg yolks and continue as per the lime mayo recipe. Taste to correct the seasoning – it may need a touch more lemon juice or a pinch of caster sugar.

BREAD & BUTTER PICKLES

MAKES 1 X 1-LITRE JAR

Gherkins, cornichons and pickled cucumbers of any kind work so well with fish. These bread and butter pickles offer a serious crunch and are as sweet as they are sour. They're the perfect accompaniment to fried or battered fish, especially when there is a little heat involved.

1 tsp coriander seeds

175g caster sugar

175ml apple cider vinegar

½ tsp ground turmeric

½ tsp fine sea salt

2 cucumbers

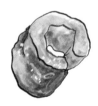

Start by making your pickle solution, as it has to cool before you add your cucumbers. Put a small heavy-based saucepan on a low heat. Add the coriander seeds and toast them lightly, keeping the pan moving, for 1 minute. Add the sugar, vinegar, turmeric and salt and mix to combine with a small whisk.

Increase the heat to medium-high and bring to the boil to make sure the sugar dissolves. Remove the pan from the heat and allow to cool completely.

Top and tail the cucumbers, then cut them in half lengthways. Use a teaspoon to remove the seeds. The seeds have a higher water content and will cause your pickles to lose their crunch and bite far quicker if you leave them in.

With the inside of the cucumber face down on the chopping board, cut the cucumbers at an angle into slices 1cm thick.

Once the pickle solution is cool, add the cucumbers. Leave for a couple of hours to let the pickle solution draw the moisture out of the cucumbers. This will increase the volume of the pickle solution. Transfer to a sterilised 1-litre jar and store in the fridge, where the pickles will keep for two weeks.

Just before serving, I like to remove the pickles from the brine and mix them with a couple of chopped sprigs of fresh dill.

AGRODOLCE KETCHUP

MAKES 580G

This recipe, like most of the recipes in Goldie, was born out of necessity. We had a glut of fabulous locally grown tomatoes that we needed to preserve. Agrodolce literally means 'sweet and sour' in Italian. This recipe calls for San Marzano tomatoes, which are a fleshy tomato with a lower water content than most tomatoes, but you can use any tomato for this recipe, even canned ones – just take the time to cook off as much of that water as possible.

3 tbsp vegetable oil

1 onion, sliced

4 garlic cloves, crushed

1 tsp fine sea salt

1kg San Marzano tomatoes, diced (or see the intro)

60g light brown sugar

50ml balsamic vinegar

1 tbsp Highbank Orchard Organic Apple Treacle (or regular treacle)

1 tbsp Goldie house hot sauce (page 65) or Tabasco

1 tbsp apple cider vinegar

½ tsp smoked paprika

Heat the oil in a medium-sized heavy-based saucepan on a medium-low heat. Add the onion, garlic and salt and cook for 5 minutes, until softened.

Add the diced tomatoes and increase the heat to medium-high. Cook for 15 minutes, stirring regularly, until the base of the pan begins to catch. The higher the water content in the tomatoes you use, the longer you'll have to cook them at this stage to cook off as much water as possible.

Once the base of the pan begins to catch, reduce the heat to medium-low. Add the brown sugar, balsamic vinegar, treacle, hot sauce, vinegar and smoked paprika and cook for a further 5 minutes. Remove the pan from the heat and allow to cool slightly.

Once cooled, blend the ketchup in a food processor or with a hand blender. Transfer to a sterilised 1-litre jar and allow to cool completely, then refrigerate. This ketchup will keep well in the fridge for a month.

BLOOD ORANGE KOSHO

MAKES 1 X 220G JAR

Kosho is a Japanese condiment typically made with the zest of the citrus fruit yuzu, fresh chilli and salt and it's usually served with sashimi. Blood oranges are one of my favourite ingredients to work with, so when they are in season, I'm always looking for ways to preserve their unique flavour for as long as I can.

With any kosho, a little goes a very long way due to its high salt content. Anoint sliced raw or cured fish with a little dab of this kosho, such as the dry-cured fish on page 47. I also love mixing some with unsalted butter and adding it to oysters before baking.

140g stemmed and deseeded fresh red serrano chillies

60g blood orange zest (approx. 15 oranges)

20g fine sea salt

NOTE: The chillies and zest should be weighed *after* processing – in other words, you need 140 grams of chillies *after* they've been stemmed and deseeded and 60 grams of zest *after* it's been grated.

Roughly chop the chillies. Grate the zest from the blood oranges using a fine Microplane.

Put the chopped chillies, blood orange zest and salt in a food processor and blend until it forms a rough paste. Transfer to a small sterilised jar and let it age in the fridge for two weeks before using. The kosho will keep in the fridge for six months.

GOLDIE HOUSE HOT SAUCE

MAKES 1 LITRE

This recipe is a great introduction to fermentation – it's spicy, sour and such a versatile condiment to have on hand in your kitchen. The tanginess of this sauce works so well with oysters, but it's also great in marinades, salsas and over eggs. It's worth taking the time to make a big batch of this sauce as it doesn't last long!

1kg stemmed and deseeded fresh red serrano chillies

2 garlic cloves, crushed

20g fine sea salt

NOTE: The chillies should be weighed *after* processing – in other words, you need 1kg of chillies *after* they've been stemmed and deseeded.

Roughly chop the stemmed and deseeded chillies, then put them in a large mixing bowl with the crushed garlic and salt.

Wearing a pair of kitchen gloves, massages the chillies and garlic with the salt. This will begin to extract water from the chillies, producing a brine which will allow for fermentation. Massage for 5 minutes, allow to sit for 15 minutes, then massage again for a further 5 minutes.

Transfer all the contents of the bowl to a sterilised 1-litre jar with a lid and leave in a cool, dark place for two weeks. Open or 'burp' the jar every day or so to allow the gases from the fermentation process to escape. I always like to do this in a sink in case there are any overflows.

After two weeks have passed, tip all the contents of the jar into a food processor and blend on full speed to produce a vibrant red sauce. You might need a little water to achieve the right consistency, but no more than 100ml.

At this stage you can add a little sugar and/or apple cider vinegar depending on your preference, but I like to leave the sauce as it is.

Pour the sauce into sterilised jars and refrigerate for up to three months.

INDEX

Nine Bean Rows

23 Mountjoy Square

Dublin, D01 E0F8

Ireland

@9beanrowsbooks

ninebeanrowsbooks.com

NINE
BEAN
ROWS

Blasta Books is an imprint of Nine Bean Rows Books Ltd.

@blastabooks blastabooks.com

First published 2024

Text copyright © Aishling Moore, 2024

Illustrations copyright © Nicky Hooper, 2024

ISBN: 978-1-7392105-4-0

Editor: Kristin Jensen

Series artist: Nicky Hooper
nickyhooper.com

Designer: Jane Matthews
janematthewsdesign.com

Proofreader: Jocelyn Doyle

Printed by L&C Printing Group, Poland

The paper in this book is produced using pulp from managed forests.

About the author

Aishling Moore is one of Ireland's most exciting young chefs. Her fish restaurant, Goldie, in Cork's city centre, has pioneered gill-to-fin cooking in Ireland. By adopting a whole-catch approach, the restaurant allows what's landed to dictate what's served.

Goldie opened in late 2019. That same year, Aishling was named Chef of the Year by John and Sally McKenna. Goldie achieved Michelin Bib Gourmand status in 2021 and in 2022 was awarded Best Casual Dining in Ireland 2022 by both *Food & Wine Magazine* and the Restaurant Association of Ireland. In 2023, Aishling was named the *Food & Wine Magazine* Young Chef of the Year and also became deputy head of the Euro-Toques Ireland Food Council, an organisation that endeavours to preserve Irish culinary heritage by supporting traditional cooking methods and promoting producers of local and seasonal artisan products.

@aishlingmoore